LET US ADORE HIM

LET US ADORE HIM
Daily Reflections for Advent and Christmas

Richard N. Fragomeni

Franciscan
MEDIA
Cincinnati, Ohio

Cover and book design by Mark Sullivan

LIBRARY OF CONGRESS CATALOGING-IN-PUBLICATION DATA
Fragomeni, Richard N.
Let us adore Him : daily reflections for Advent and Christmas / Fr. Richard Fragomeni.
pages cm
ISBN 978-1-61636-666-7 (alk. paper)
1. Advent—Meditations. 2. Christmas—Meditations. 3. Common lectionary (1992) I. Title.
BV40.F73 2014
242'.33—dc23
2014016009
ISBN 978-1-61636-666-7

Published by Franciscan Media
28 W. Liberty St.
Cincinnati, OH 45202
www.FranciscanMedia.org

Printed in the United States of America.
Printed on acid-free paper.
14 15 16 17 18 5 4 3 2 1

CONTENTS

*To my students at Catholic Theological Union
—past and present.*

*And to Mike Hay, who celebrated Advent
and Christmas well.*

THE COMMUNION ANTIPHONS for Advent are like a conversation: Some days we talk to God; other days Gods talks to us. You may not have had the opportunity before to hear these beautiful texts, as they are one of four options that can be used as a Communion chant for singing (or praying) during the Communion Rite. Most parishes usually sing a suitable liturgical song.

Here's what the *General Instruction of the Roman Missal* tells us about the Communion chant, which includes the Communion antiphon:

> While the Priest is receiving the Sacrament, the Communion Chant is begun, its purpose being to express the spiritual union of the communicants by means of the unity of their voices, to show gladness of heart, and to bring out more clearly the "communitarian" character of the procession to receive

the Eucharist. The singing is prolonged for as long as the Sacrament is being administered to the faithful. (86)

We will focus on these antiphons in this little book during the Advent and Christmas season. Many times the antiphons express a similar theme as the readings for the day. At other times, they take us in a different direction entirely, allowing us to explore the mystery of God more deeply.

I especially want to invite you into the "joy of heart" aspect of the antiphons, a characteristic inherent in both Advent and the Christmas season. As we go about our daily activities during Advent, we might be drawn into the various ways that, especially at this time of year, our culture says, "I will satisfy you here, this way. I will satisfy you there, that way. I can satisfy all your dreams right now and everything you desire will be fulfilled here."

Well, the reality is that nothing will ever satisfy us but the love of God. Nothing will ever tame the restlessness of our desire except the joy of heart that comes with living in God's light and sharing that light with the world.

This year, I invite you to join with me in exploring the wondrous mystery of God through the Word of our liturgy and of Scripture. There we will find the joy of heart that will enable us to be true disciples of the Word Incarnate, the Christ whose birth we remember and whose return we anticipate each year during the sacred seasons of Advent and Christmas.

Be Alert

Year A: Isaiah 2:1–5; Psalm 122:1–2, 3–4, 4–5, 6–7, 8–9;
Romans 13:11–14; Matthew 24:37–44
Year B: Isaiah 63:16b–17, 19b; 64:2–7; Psalm 80:2–3, 15–16,
18–19; 1 Corinthians 1:3–9; Mark 13:33–37
Year C: Jeremiah 33:14–16; Psalm 25:4–5, 8–9, 10, 14 (1b);
1 Thessalonians 3:12—4:2; Luke 21:25–28, 34–36

*The Lord will bestow his bounty, and our earth
shall yield its increase.*

IN THE WEEKS before Advent, the readings talk of end times, when the world will fall apart. Yet there is a tension in those readings, because God is going to create a brand new world with the birth of Jesus. This talk of end times lingers in today's Gospel for Year C, Luke 21:25–28, 34–36: "There will be signs in the sun, the moon, and the stars, and on the earth distress among nations confused by the roaring of the sea and the waves. People will faint from fear and foreboding of what is coming upon the world, for the powers of the heavens will be shaken."

The Gospel concludes with a caution: "Be alert at all times, praying that you may have the strength to escape all these things that will take place, and to stand before the Son of Man." Be alert. In fact, this theme is repeated in both Gospels for today: "Beware, keep alert; for you do not know when the time will come" (Mark 13:33), and "Keep awake therefore, for you do not know on what day your Lord is coming" (Matthew 24:42). For what are we keeping awake, alert?

The answer is in today's Communion antiphon: "The Lord will bestow his bounty, and our earth shall yield its increase." From the destruction of the earth will come the new creation, Jesus Christ. We stand with full expectation that the Savior will bring his just rewards to the people. This is why we keep alert, stay awake.

Advent is about the One who comes to overwhelm us beyond our wildest dreams with what God has in store for those who wait in joyful hope. So keep awake, wait on the Lord, and pray with expectation that the earth will yield its full bounty when we celebrate the birth of Jesus this Christmas.

PRACTICE

What is your most profound hope and expectation this Advent?

Welcome In

Isaiah 2:1–5; Psalm 122:1–2, 3–4, (4–5, 6–7) 8–9;
Matthew 8:5–11

Come, O Lord, visit us in peace,
that we may rejoice before you
with a blameless heart.

THERE IS A peace down deep inside that we are all looking for in a turbulent and troubled world. The Communion antiphon for this Monday of the first week of Advent speaks very clearly of that desire for peace. It is also an invitation to the Lord, that he visit us.

To invite someone to visit you demands that you give them access; you have to let that person in. When someone visits your home, for instance, you have to unlock your door and welcome him or her in for a cup of tea. When you go to see someone in the hospital, you have to get the necessary permissions to enter the person's room, especially if they are in the intensive care unit.

Giving someone access demands a disposition of heart, what the great spiritual writers describe as surrender, a yielding, placing no resistance to the entry of the guest. The blameless heart is the heart that knows how to yield, how to surrender, how to give of itself. It is the heart that lets go, the heart that forgives, the heart that ultimately loves. In that opening of the heart, the guest will enter and peace will be given, even in the most turbulent of times and situations.

In our troubled hearts we know for sure that we cannot be the answer to our own questions, the answer to our own peace. And so in Advent we cry out, "Come, O come Emmanuel! Come, visit us and bring your peace to hearts filled with the cares and troubles of our lives. Let us become a holding place for you as we begin this blessed season."

PRACTICE

Reflect on an area of your life where you long for peace. What can you do this Advent to prepare a place in your heart where the Christ child can bring his peace?

Full of Keen Desire

Isaiah 11:1–10; Psalm 72:1, 7–8, 12–13, 17; Luke 10:21–24

The Just Judge will bestow a crown of righteousness on those who eagerly await his coming.

What is a crown of righteousness? This symbol is used to convey a royal dignity that we are given at baptism and confirmation, when our heads are anointed with holy chrism, just as Jesus was anointed priest, prophet, and king.

The coming of Christ celebrated each Advent is three-fold: the coming of Christ in the past, in Bethlehem; the coming of Christ in the future, which we anticipate at the end of time; and the coming of Christ that we receive and share in the present. In reality, we participate in the threefold coming of Christ every time we receive Holy Communion. And as we await and receive his presence in Eucharist, we do so with the crown of righteousness placed upon our heads at baptism. Like Jesus, we are made a royal priesthood, a holy nation, a people set apart.

An important word in today's Communion antiphon is the adverb *eagerly*. Not only do we await the coming of Jesus, but we await it eagerly, with *eros*, with passion. When you examine the origins with the word *eagerly*, you see that it can mean strenuously, ardently, fiercely, forcefully. But the definition I like best is "full of keen desire."

Above all else, our keenest desire is to come to know the Christ who, as a just judge, comes to us in mercy and humility, in communion with us with his Body and Blood. With Jesus, who first came among us as an infant, we wait for the fulfillment of that coming when God will become all in all.

PRACTICE
How keen is your desire to intimately know Jesus? This Advent season, may that desire be stoked so that as we eagerly await his coming we may fully know who we are as royal people.

An Enlightened Eye

Isaiah 25:6–10; Psalm 23:1–3, 3–4, 5, 6; Matthew 15:29–37

Behold, our Lord will come with power
and will enlighten the eyes of his servants.

When the Scripture uses the word *eyes*, it can mean several things. First, it can mean the eyes that are located in our skulls, the visual eyes, the eyes of the sense of sight. We have these eyes so that we can see in the world the beauty and the wonder of creation.

But there is another understanding of eyes in Scripture—the eye of the heart, the inner eye. The inner eye sees and understands the depth of things. As St. Paul says in 1 Corinthians 2:9, it is the eye that has not seen what God has prepared for those who love him.

The Lord who comes to us, the presence of Christ who abides in us, will enlighten our eyes. I would like to suggest it is both the inner eye of the heart as well as the outer eyes that are indeed enlightened, so we can see everything in the interconnectivity and greatness of God's power. The enlightened eye can see, as Paul further says in Galatians 3:28, that "There is no longer Jew or Greek, there is no longer slave or free, there is no longer male and female; for all of you are one in Christ Jesus."

With the enlightened eye, we no longer see the distinctions that create divisions; rather, we celebrate the distinctions as the various ways in which God's power is made manifest. With the enlightened eye, we see everything as one.

The power referred to in the Communion antiphon for today is the power of God's grace. It is the grace that we surrender to, the grace that can transform our eyes so everything we see and perceive within it reflects the movement and presence of God. And in that presence we rejoice.

PRACTICE
Where do your eyes need enlightenment today?

Living Justly

ISAIAH 26:1–6; PSALM 118:1, 8–9, 19–21, 25–27A;
MATTHEW 7:21, 24–27

Let us live justly and devoutly in this age,
as we await the blessed hope
and the coming of the glory of our great God.

WHEN BENEDICT XVI, our pope emeritus, was editing
the third edition of the Roman Missal, he added several
parts to it himself. One of those parts is the dismissal
often used, in which the deacon or the priest says to
the assembly, "Go in peace, glorifying the Lord by your
life." This is a good way to summarize our Advent
meditation today.

On a practical basis, how do we justly and devoutly
glorify the Lord with our lives as we await this blessed
hope, the coming of our great God? Simply this: It
means that we offer to one another what is due to one
another.

Scripture tells us that what is justly due to one another
is that we love one another as God loves us. Further,

we are *commanded*—a very strong word, but true—to glorify the Lord. Glorifying God is not the devotion simply of gathering for Church celebrations or lighting our Advent wreaths. The glory God desires is that our hearts be filled with the justice that renders to others the kind of love and service modeled by Jesus.

If someone is hungry we give them something to eat; if someone is thirsty we give them something to drink. If we are living in unjust systems that use tyranny to offend and oppress the least of our brothers and sisters, we engage in the transformation of those systems. In so doing, we glorify the Lord by our lives.

This life of justice is the true devotion of the heart. To live that profound justice in this present age bears witness to the fact that we are a people of blessed hope, wayfarers who expect with keen desire the glory of God.

PRACTICE

Whom do you know that needs something to eat or drink, or help in overcoming an oppression?

Changed and Glorified

ISAIAH 29:17–24; PSALM 27:1, 4, 13–14; MATTHEW 9:27–31

We await a savior, the Lord Jesus Christ,
who will change our mortal bodies,
to conform with his glorified body.

NOT TOO LONG ago in Catholic practice, every Friday during the year was considered a day of fasting and abstinence, a day to remember what happened on that first Good Friday, when Christ saved us and redeemed us with his own Body on the cross.

Today we also remember that Christ's glorious Body is meant to be an opportunity for our own bodies to be changed and glorified. We come to Eucharist with the hope of a Savior, the Lord Jesus Christ, who will change our mortal bodies to conform with his glorified Body— the Body of his death, his Resurrection, his ascended glory into heaven, the Body of Christ that now fills the universe and all its parts, the Body of Christ that transforms mortality into the promise of an abundant life, a resurrected life without end.

In Advent we pray that we will be transformed, changed in a twinkling of an eye by Christ. Certainly each time we share in his Body and Blood in the Eucharist we are changed by the experience of sharing in his Communion. St. Augustine notes that when we share in Holy Communion it is we who are changed; it is not we who take the Body of Christ into us, but we are taken into the glorified Body.

This first Friday of Advent, as we wait in joyful hope for the coming of our Savior, we are all invited to allow Christ to conform us, to change us, to transform us, to rethink our own lives because Christ points us into a unique way of being. Even now, we celebrate that we have been changed and that these mortal bodies already have become a sacramental demonstration to others that Christ has done good work in us.

PRACTICE

How can we allow Christ to change us even more deeply into the image of his glorified self?

The Gift of Mercy

ISAIAH 30:19–21, 23–26; PSALM 147:1–2, 3–4, 5–6;
MATTHEW 9:35—10:1, 6–8

Behold, I am coming soon
and my recompense is with me, says the Lord,
to bestow a reward according to the deeds of each.

TODAY CHRIST IS speaking with us from the book of Revelation: "See, I am coming soon; my reward is with me, to repay according to everyone's work" (22:12).

What is interesting here is that what will be bestowed is a reward—not a punishment but a reward, according to the deeds of each. We certainly know what to expect when our deeds are good, but what do we expect when Christ brings this recompense of a reward according to our deeds—not all of which are good?

I would suggest that this is Advent hope: that the One who is coming soon—indeed, the One whom we receive in Communion each time we participate in liturgy—will be present with us in the richness of the now and the moment in which we live and breathe. This

Christ who is coming will bestow on us a recompense of reward according to our deeds.

A few years ago, I met an elderly priest, then approaching ninety, who said this: "As I am getting older I am not getting much better. But I sure am trusting more in God's mercy." As I myself grow older, I share this priest's sense that I am not getting better. But in that process I am becoming more and more assured of the mercy of God.

The reward that Christ will bring is the reward of a divine mercy that enters into the chaos of our lives. Christ is bringing to all of us, all sinners, the reward of a mercy so great that no matter what we have done or what we have failed to do, we are shown the mercy that helps us know and understand we all are worth more than our actions.

PRACTICE
Pray that God's mercy fills an area of your heart where it is most needed. Are you ready to receive such a gift?

How to Climb a Mountain

YEAR A: ISAIAH 11:1–10; PSALM 72:1–2, 7–8, 12–13, 17 (SEE 7);
ROMANS 15:4–9; MATTHEW 2:1–2
YEAR B: ISAIAH 40:1–5, 9–11; PSALM 85:9–10, 11–12, 13–14 (8);
2 PETER 3:8–14; MARK 1:1–8
YEAR C: BARUCH 5:1–9; PSALM 126:1–2, 2–3, 4–5, 6 (3);
PHILIPPIANS 1:4–6, 8–11; LUKE 3:1–6

*Jerusalem, arise and stand upon the heights,
and behold the joy which comes to you from God.*

WE ARE CALLED to climb a mountain this Advent
season. We can do that in several ways. First, we climb
it by being attentive to every step, being mindful of who
we are and who we are called to be by God's grace. It
is the mindfulness of staying awake, because we cannot
climb the heights of a mountain without paying attention. Otherwise, we will stumble and fall.

The second way we are called to climb the mountain is to recognize and become conscious of the ways
in which we do fall, how it is we manage to sink into
the depths of the netherworld, the depths of sin. Being
attentive also means being able to name and identify the

great sins that keep us from beholding the glory of God.

There are seven great sins, capital sins, really, that we need to be aware of. Can you name them? Jealousy is the sin of envy and craving for someone else's goods, someone else's lifestyle, someone else's way of being. Gluttony is overconsumption of something: too much food, too much work, too much time with social media. With the sin of lust we addictively desire physical pleasure, whether sexual or emotional. Sloth is a laziness that keeps us from recognizing that our task is to be laborers in the vineyard. Pride is the lack of the awareness of who we truly are because we are living in our false identities. Wrath, the kind of anger that keeps us from knowing that all is gift, creates war and violence within our families, our neighborhoods, and our world.

But the ultimate capital sin that keeps us from rising to the top of the mountain is avarice, or greed, the desire to clutch and hold on to everyone and everything. It keeps us caught up in an economic system that is competitive rather than cooperative.

The Second Sunday of Advent invites us to go deeper into the place where we come to know that only God can give us joy beyond all understanding. To climb to those heights, we have to pay attention to where we are going—as well as to where we do not want to go.

PRACTICE
Which of the capital sins keeps you from climbing to the heights of Jerusalem?

The Power of Three

ISAIAH 35:1–10; PSALM 85:9–10, 11–12, 13–14; LUKE 5:17–26

Come, O Lord, visit us in peace,
that we may rejoice before you with a blameless heart.

AS WE BEGIN this second week of Advent, something interesting happens. It is called the "power of three" because during the next two weeks, from Monday through Saturday, the same Communion antiphons are used as in the first week. For the first three weeks of Advent, therefore, we approach the Eucharistic table singing the same song over and over again.

The power of three is an important dynamic, not just in religion but in many contexts. We often hear people say that good things come in threes or there will be three deaths all at once; in baseball there are three strikes, and you're out. And certainly there is the three-fold celebration of the presence of God, Father, Son, and Holy Spirit, the Trinity.

In the Hebrew language, the superlative form of an adjective was represented by three iterations. For instance when we say "Holy, holy, holy" it means "holy, holier, holiest." And so the Communion antiphons for the first three weeks of Advent are repeated as if to tell us that something is important here, get it right. Good things come in threes; our invitation to grace this Advent comes in three.

The antiphon today, which we read last Monday as well, says: "Come, O Lord, visit us in peace that we may rejoice before you with a blameless heart." As we prepare for Christmas we are asked to reflect on the three comings of Christ: his birth in Bethlehem, his coming at the end of time, and his coming in the present time through the gift of Holy Communion, the Body and Blood of Christ. In each of these comings we prepare to receive our royal guest with a blameless heart.

PRACTICE
How do you need to be purified this Advent so that you can receive Jesus with a blameless heart?

Three Crowns

ISAIAH 40:1–11; PSALM 96:1–2, 3, 10, 11–12, 13;
MATTHEW 18:12–14

*The Just Judge will bestow a crown of righteousness
on those who eagerly await his coming.*

IN ADVENT WE celebrate Jesus coming to us in the past, in the present, and in the future. This "power of three" also invites us to see there are three kinds of crowns that we are offered by God.

The first is the crown of royalty. At baptism, the crowns of our heads are anointed with chrism, and, like Christ, we become part of a royal priesthood. We become a people that have been crowned with the glory of the sovereign Lord of the universe, who calls us to be part of this universe and to engage in its wonder and its glory as we await his joyful coming, again.

The second crown is the stephanos, made of something alive, like the laurel leaves that make up the crowns used for winning Olympians. Throughout the history of the Church we have been invited to be champions on the course to God, to be champions who, like St. Paul, run the race (see 2 Timothy 4:7). During these Advent days we are called to run toward Christmas, not with all the commercial trappings but as the feast of the Incarnation where we are identified more deeply with Christ.

Christ also gives us a third crown, and that is the crown of thorns. Those who await the coming of the Lord, those who share in Holy Communion, those who come to this table singing this antiphon acknowledge that we receive the One who has died for us. We echo this in the Memorial Acclamation that states, "When we eat this bread and drink this cup we proclaim your death, O Lord." The crown of thorns invites us to share in the suffering of Christ and to embrace the cross. In doing so, we share in the crown of victory of Christ.

PRACTICE

Advent invites us to wear all three crowns. Which crown do you resist the most?

Three Ways to See

Isaiah 40:25–31; Psalm 103:1–2, 3–4, 8, 10; Matthew 11:28–30

*Behold, our Lord will come with power
and will enlighten the eyes of his servants.*

LET'S CONTINUE WITH the notion of the power of three and take a look at the three kinds of eyes that God can enlighten in us.

The first eye is the eye of the body. So many times we look at something but do not savor it, rejoice in it, engage with it. Advent is an invitation to ask God to enlighten the eyes of our bodies so that we can see a snowflake and a child's expression, and know the beauty and wonder of creation.

We also have the eyes of the mind, the mind's eye. With these we have the ability to think, to reason, to rationalize. With the eyes of our mind we are able to do mathematics and calculus equations. It is the mind's eye that is able to delve into the imagination, to create and dream of possibilities.

The third kind of eye is the eye of the heart, the eye of the spirit. With the eyes of the heart we can perceive what is invisible to eyes of the body and the mind's eye. As Antoine de Saint-Exupéry says in his book *The Little Prince*, "It is only with the heart that one can see rightly. What is essential is invisible to the eye." With the eyes of the spirit we no longer see bread and wine, but appreciate that here is the living presence of Christ. We see a baby in a manger and we know that God so loved the world he gave it his only Son.

We ask the God of Advent to illuminate all three eyes so that the One who comes, the One who we behold, will enlighten us in all three ways.

PRACTICE

Sit quietly with your eyes closed, for five to ten minutes. Open the eyes of your spirit, and see what becomes visible.

Virtuous Living

ISAIAH 41:13–20; PSALM 145:1, 9, 10–11, 12–13;
MATTHEW 11:11–15

*Let us live justly and devoutly in this age,
as we await the blessed hope
and the coming of the glory of our great God.*

TODAY WE'LL FOCUS on three words from the antiphon—
justly, *devoutly*, and *hope*—with a reflection on the great
theological virtues of faith, hope, and love.

Faith is the devoted heart surrendering completely
and in trust to God. It is not the same as belief because
you can have many beliefs but no faith. We are to devote
our entire life to being surrendered over to God, to
yielding ourselves completely into God. May we learn
to live with that much devout faith.

Then we are invited to live in the blessed hope and
the coming of the glory of our great God. After we
say the Lord's Prayer at Mass, the priest prays, "as we
await our blessed hope and the coming of our Savior,
Jesus Christ." This blessed hope is an invitation for us

not to have a hope that is merely expectation charged with a great emotion, but to have the kind of hope that is an openness to whatever life brings, a delight in the surprises that God has in store for those who love. It is indeed a willingness to see as gift all that we receive in our lives.

Finally, we are invited to live justly. The justice of God and the virtue of love—*agape*—are intermeshed. This love is not the same as an emotional feeling, but is rather the unbelievable experience of communion. Justice is one and the same with *agape*. This sense of deep communion means that we are able to love our neighbor as ourselves because we recognize that we and our neighbor are one in the love that unites us, in the hope that surprises us, and in the devotion that calls us to surrender ourselves completely to God.

PRACTICE

How can you live more justly, devoutly, and in hope this Advent?

Vulnerable and Mighty

ISAIAH 48:17–19; PSALM 1:1–2, 3, 4, 6; MATTHEW 11:16–19

We await a savior, the Lord Jesus Christ,
who will change our mortal bodies,
to conform with his glorified body.

As WE ONCE again approach Friday, we remember that day when the cross became our hope and the portal through which our mortal bodies can be transformed into the glorified Body of Christ.

Each year on Good Friday, as the Church comes to venerate the cross of Christ, the crucified One, a Greek song is sung. It is in three parts, actually. It says *Agios O Theos*, "Holy is God"; *Agios ischyros*, "Holy and Mighty is God"; *Agios athantos eleison imas*, "Holy and Immortal One, have mercy upon us." Each of these three refrains is sung over and over during the liturgy.

We say "Holy is our God," which means that our God is wholly other and wholly one of us, true God, and true human, who invites us into holiness of life. This holiness is given to us as *ischyros*, meaning "might." But the

mightiness of our God is portrayed in weakness, a crucified Body on the cross. Our holiness is given to us in
vulnerability and in pain, in the magnitude of suffering
and love shared with us by Jesus Christ.

The third refrain on Good Friday, *agios athanatos*,
suggests the deathless One, the immortal Christ. And
so we come to the Communion table knowing that
Jesus, who took on human form, who lived and died on
the cross, rose again to give us eternal life. This is the
vulnerability of the One who feeds us with bread and
wine during this Advent season, the immortality that
Christ shares with us celebrated in giving us this gift
of his Body and Blood. In this we become mighty in
our weakness, living in communion with God and one
another as we await the Savior, the Lord Jesus Christ.

PRACTICE

What area of vulnerability in your life can be used to
bring you closer to God this Advent?

Here and Now

SIRACH 48:1–4, 9–11; PSALM 80:2–3, 15–16, 18–19;
MATTHEW 17:10–13

Behold, I am coming soon
and my recompense is with me, says the Lord,
to bestow a reward according to the deeds of each.

WHAT DOES IT mean that the Lord is coming "soon"?
We divide time into the past, the present, and the future.
When we look for something to come soon, it is as if
we are anticipating something with a memory of the
past. And always the past and the future somehow get
entwined with the present moment, the here and now.

One of the most popular Memorial Acclamations
in the previous translation of the Roman Missal celebrated this: "Christ has died, Christ is risen, Christ will
come again." During Advent, we prepare to celebrate
the Christ who came in the past, in Bethlehem; Christ
who will come in the future to bring us recompense
according to our deeds; and Christ who is with us in

now, most uniquely in the living presence of Christ in the gift of Eucharist.

The Advent season invites us to recognize that the coming of Christ is to come, yes, but it is also already here. In this mystery of the past, present, and future we experience in this moment, here and now, the living God. Spiritual teachers and Christian mystics throughout the centuries all point to this moment, this eternal "now" moment where the past and the present and the future are woven together in the living experience of God among us.

Immersed in the wonder of this here and now moment, we are then able to be fully alive and face whatever it is we need to deal with, knowing that we are not alone. In this way, when the One who is coming soon arrives, we will be ready to greet him and embrace him with open arms because we have been doing it all along.

PRACTICE

How do you most fully experience Christ in the here and now?

Finding Joy

YEAR A: ISAIAH 35:1–6A, 10; PSALM 146:6–7, 8–9, 9–10;
JAMES 5:7–10; MATTHEW 11:2–11
YEAR B: ISAIAH 61:1–2A, 10–11; LUKE 1:46–48, 49–50, 53–54;
1 THESSALONIANS 5:16–24; JOHN 1:6–8, 19–28
YEAR C: ZEPHANIAH 3:14–18A; PSALM 12:2–3, 4, 5–6;
PHILIPPIANS 4:4–7; LUKE 3:10–18

*Say to the faint of heart: Be strong
and do not fear.
Behold, our God will come, and he will save us.*

THE THIRD SUNDAY of Advent is traditionally known as
Gaudete Sunday, a time to "Rejoice in the Lord always;
again I will say, Rejoice" (Philippians 4:4). We rejoice
because Christmas is close at hand.

This Sunday of rejoicing causes me to pause and ask:
Why are we faint of heart to begin with? One answer is
this: because we live in a succession of opposites. We live
in good times and bad times, in sickness and in health.
And in these successions we find ourselves being tossed
around by pleasure and pain, loss and gain, praise and
blame, fame and disgrace. And because we are tossed

around like this, we often find ourselves happy one day and sad the next day.

But on this Sunday in the middle of the wonderful season of Advent, we are told to rejoice, to be strong, to not be afraid for behold, our God will save us. And oddly enough, the way God saves us is indeed by putting us in the middle of pleasure and pain, loss and gain, praise and blame, fame and disgrace. God says, "Stay with me here in the center of all these opposites. Here in this center I will give you freedom from the back and forth, the pleasure and pain, the loss and gain, the praise and blame. In this center you will find joy, which is ability to say yes in the midst of life's ups and downs."

PRACTICE

What keeps you from experiencing joy in the midst of the ups and downs of life?

Missionaries of Good News

NUMBERS 24:2–7, 15–17A; PSALM 25:4–5; 6–7; 8–9;
MATTHEW 21:23–27

Come, O Lord, visit us in peace,
that we may rejoice before you
with a blameless heart.

EACH DAY OF the liturgical year, the Church commemorates holy men and women, known for their gift of living in the Lord with the kind of open joy we share in these days before Christmas. In the next few meditations, we'll look at some of these saints whose feast days we celebrate in Advent.

We celebrate St. Francis Xavier's feast day on December 3. In peace and with a blameless heart, he went to Asia to proclaim the Good News; this was his mission. Francis was born in Spain in 1506. Together with Ignatius of Loyola, he was one of the original founders of the Jesuit Order. He was a messenger of Christianity who went to India and Japan, baptized many people in Asia and brought them to the faith, and died on his way to China in 1552.

Francis Xavier is an example for us in two ways. First, he encourages us to be courageous and creative in sharing the Good News of Jesus Christ with others in our own times, because this is what he did in the sixteenth century with the newly founded Jesuit charism. He went out to Asia and creatively discovered a way to proclaim the gospel.

Second, Francis Xavier fulfilled his mission fearlessly and unreservedly, without compromise and without distraction. He was a man of blameless heart. It is often difficult for us as husbands and wives, as parents and as single people, as young and as old, to minister in the face of the many distractions in our lives.

But the heart of Francis Xavier was fixed on only one thing: Having come to know the Lord, his only desire was to share the Good News of Jesus Christ with others. And in sharing that Good News with others, he became the patron of all the missions.

PRACTICE

How do you share the Good News with others?

Generous St. Nick

ZEPHANIAH 3:1–2, 9–13; PSALM 34:2–3, 6–7, 17–18, 19, 23;
MATTHEW 21:28–32

*The Just Judge will bestow a crown of righteousness
on those who eagerly await his coming.*

ST. NICHOLAS, WHOSE is feast day is December 6, was
born in the third century. Although he was a layperson,
he was named a bishop because of his great holiness,
and he became an example of extraordinary goodness
and generosity.

The legends of St. Nicholas and the miracles that are
attributed to him are numerous and notable. One tells
of how he saved three sisters. Because they came from a
poor family, the girls had no dowry to use to be married,
and as such their only option was either prostitution
or slavery. Nicholas heard of their plight, and over the
course of three nights threw a bag of gold, one for each
daughter, into the window of their father's house.

Another tells of a time when the crops in Myra failed,
and a famine came on the land. At the same time, in

Italy, a merchant was loading his ship with grain to sell in Egypt. That night, as he slept, Nicholas appeared to the merchant in a dream and pledged a payment of three gold coins if he came to Myra to sell the grain. When he awoke, the merchant found three gold coins in his hand, and he immediately sailed to Myra where his grain saved the people from famine.

During his lifetime, Nicholas became generous as Christ was generous. He humbly wore the crown of righteousness. This is the secret of Nicholas and his role as inspiration for Santa Claus. As we await Christ's coming may we become like Nicholas and be Santa Claus for others by the generosity of our own lives. Our gifts at Christmas, be they large or small, are signs of the greatest gift of all: Jesus born among us, as flesh and blood.

PRACTICE

What does the tradition of Santa Claus mean to you? How does it enhance or distract from your observance of Christmas?

The Immaculate Conception

ISAIAH 45:6–8, 18, 21–25; PSALM 85:9–10, 11–12, 13–14;
LUKE 7:18–23

Behold, our Lord will come with power
and will enlighten the eyes of his servants.

WE ASK GOD to enlighten our eyes, that they may be pure and clear and focused. As such, we remember today the Immaculate Conception of Mary, which we celebrate on December 8. The Immaculate Conception celebrates the grace-filled being whom we acknowledge as the Mother of God and our Mother, Mary Immaculate.

The Doctrine of the Immaculate Conception was proclaimed by Blessed Pope Pius IX in the year 1854 and teaches that, from the moment of her conception, Mary was without sin. In Europe, this was the era of the Enlightenment, a movement whereby European philosophy and European governments were driven by the belief that science would be our savior. It was a rationale proclaiming that the perfect human being, the perfect social order, the perfect reality could be created by the human mind and science.

During the Enlightenment, religion was considered superstition that would be replaced by science. It would be a new era of creating perfect human beings by social order, scientific investigation, and the enlightenment of the human mind. Nowadays, we know that this was a false belief. The attempt at forming a perfect race, a perfect human being, through science and without religion has created more hatred, more violence, more war, more destruction of humans and of the planet than has ever occurred in history to this point.

Science and the enlightened mind are indeed wonderful gifts, but true enlightenment can only come from God. The Feast of the Immaculate Conception celebrates not only the moment of Mary's conception, but at a much deeper level, a more profound level of faith, the Good News that grace alone can create the perfect humanity. God's grace alone can enlighten our eyes, the eyes of the servants. God's grace alone can transform humanity and all creation.

PRACTICE

Where do you need God's grace and enlightenment today?

Our Lady of Guadalupe

ISAIAH 54:1–10; PSALM 30:2, 4, 5–6, 11–12, 13; LUKE 7:24–30

Let us live justly and devoutly in this age,
as we await the blessed hope
and the coming of the glory of our great God.

AS WE PRAY the words "let us live justly and devoutly in this age," we note another dimension of the Holy Mother, Our Lady of Guadalupe, whose feast is celebrated on December 12.

The glory of our great God is consistently revealed in a language that we can understand. God spoke to Moses through a burning bush. He spoke to the Israelites on a smoky mountain and in a pillar of fire. He spoke to the prophets by inner voices and quiet whispers. He spoke to the shepherds through the voices of the angels, and to the Magi, who were astrologers, through an extraordinary star whose "language" they could understand.

In this same wonderful way, God's glory was revealed to Juan Diego in a language that could be understood by the poor. In Mexico, 1531, Juan Diego encountered a young girl on a hillside in Tepeyac, Mexico. She spoke to him in his own tongue, dressed in the clothing of the native people, and asked him to have a church built on the hillside in her name. Through her words and in her dress, Juan Diego recognized the girl as the Virgin Mary.

God's will was revealed through Mary to an incredulous bishop as flowers spilled from Juan Diego's cape, miraculously imprinted with an image of the Virgin appearing as an Aztec princess, so that the glory of God might be revealed to the poor and the brokenhearted in a language that speaks to them. The glory of God is not some far off glory, but a glory that is close enough for us to see and touch with enlightened eyes and hearts. Keep awake, because it comes in places we least expect and in the simple ways we can easily miss.

PRACTICE

How have you heard God speaking to you this Advent?

St. Lucy: Living in the Light

ISAIAH 56:1–3, 6–8; PSALM 67:2–3, 5, 7–8; JOHN 5:33–36

We await a savior, the Lord Jesus Christ,
who will change our mortal bodies,
to conform with his glorified body.

WHEN WE THINK about the glorified Body of Christ we might look at the account of the Transfiguration (see Matthew 17:1–6; Mark 9:2–10; Luke 9:28–36) that we find in the Gospels. Jesus climbs a mountain with Peter, James, and John, and there his garments become as white as snow and his radiance as bright as the sun. It is a luminosity so tremendous that in it is seen the fulfillment of the law and the prophets.

St. Lucy, whose name means "light," was a young virgin martyr who died in Syracuse, Sicily, around the beginning of the fourth century. She was betrothed to be married but refused to do so because she wanted to give herself completely over to serving the Lord and the poor. And so she was imprisoned, tortured, and put to death. There are numerous legends about Lucy, most prominently about her eyes being torn out. All of these stories, however, point to her inner vision, the strength of the light Lucy had within her.

Lucy's feast is December 13, a day once considered to be the winter solstice. In Scandinavian countries and other parts of the world, customs and traditions have sprung up to celebrate the feast day of St. Lucy. These practices are associated with light and celebration, for the solstice means the darkness will slowly begin turning to light.

During these Advent days, Lucy becomes for us an exemplar of what it means to have our eyes enlightened by Christ, to live in such complete dedication that nothing can separate us from Christ. Like Lucy, we will be given the light of Christ that can, even in the face of suffering, allow us, like her, to stand strong and proclaim the beauty and wonder of a God whom we have yet to see.

PRACTICE
Light a candle today and pray for those who are blind in body, mind, or heart.

The Rose Born of Mary

YEAR A: ISAIAH 7:10–14; PSALM 24:1–2, 3–4, 5–6 (7C, 10B);
ROMANS 1:1–7; MATTHEW 1:18–24
YEAR B: 2 SAMUEL 7:1–5, 8B–12, 14A, 16; PSALM 89:2–3, 4–5, 27, 29;
ROMANS 16:25–27; LUKE 1:26–38 YEAR C: MICAH 5:1–4A; PSALM
80:2–3, 15–16, 18–19; HEBREWS 10:5–10; LUKE 1:39–45

Behold, a Virgin shall conceive and bear a son;
and his name will be called Emmanuel.

THE ANTIPHON FOR today is a quote from Isaiah (7:14). Often on this day, a kind of an Advent/Christmas carol is sung in our parishes, "Lo, How a Rose E'er Blooming," which reminds us of this great prophecy from Isaiah.

The first verse echoes the prophecy that we hear in today's Communion antiphon: "Lo, how a Rose e'er blooming from tender stem hath sprung! / Of Jesse's lineage coming, as men of old have sung." The second verse speaks specifically of Isaiah: "Isaiah 'twas foretold it, the rose I have in mind / with Mary we behold it, the Virgin Mother kind." This prophecy is about Mary giving birth to a rose, a flower from Jesse's stem.

The fourth verse of this hymn usually is not sung: "This Flower, whose fragrance tender with sweetness fills the air, / Dispels with glorious splendor the darkness everywhere; / True man, yet very God, from sin and death He saves us, / And lightens every load." This is truly what we celebrate today, that Jesus, this fragrant flower born of the root of Jesse, through Mary, becomes the fragrance of holiness, the fragrance whose name is Emmanuel.

Today we pray that this Emmanuel who enters into our chaos, who saves us from sin and death, may indeed lighten our load. As Christmas approaches let us cast upon the Lord our burdens of guilt and fear and doubt and darkness, and let the Root of Jesse, the One born of the Virgin, carry our burdens with us.

PRACTICE

What burden will you ask Jesus to share with you?

O Wisdom

GENESIS 49:2, 8–10; PSALM 72:3–4, 7–8, 17; MATTHEW 1:1–17

Behold, the Desired of all the nations will come,
and the house of the Lord will be filled with glory.

On this day, things begin to change in Advent. The weekdays from December 17 up to and including December 24 are ordered in a more direct way to help us prepare for the Nativity of the Lord. From this point on, the Communion antiphons speak of an urgent desire to come ultimately to the great communion of midnight Mass where we celebrate once again the birth of our Lord.

Along with these wonderful Communion antiphons, the antiphons for evening prayer in the Liturgy of the Hours begin to change as well. These are familiarly known as the "O Antiphons" because each begins with the vocative "O" (for example, "O Wisdom," "O Lord," "O Root of Jesse"). They are an urgent calling out to God. As we continue or Advent journey together we will shift gears a bit and include these O Antiphons in our daily practice.

Today's Communion antiphon expresses the yearning of a nation to be filled with glory. When there is something empty within us, we look to fill the void that we are experiencing so that we might be satisfied. The word *satisfy* comes from the Latin root *satisfacere*, which means that something is enough. When we are dissatisfied there is a desire to be filled because something—whatever that something may be—is not enough.

The Desired of the nations is Christ, God's Wisdom. Christ is the living incarnate Wisdom. As we prepare for Christmas, let us pray for the gift of wisdom to fill our hearts, to clear our minds, and to allow us to live satisfied in the fulfillment of the desire of every nation—Jesus Christ, the living Wisdom among us.

PRACTICE
Pray or sing the O Antiphon for today:
    O Wisdom of our God Most High,
    guiding creation with power and love:
    come to teach us the path of knowledge!

O Mighty Lord

Jeremiah 23:5–8; Psalm 72:1, 12–13, 18–19; Matthew 1:18–24

His name will be called Emmanuel,
which means God-with-us.

THE ADVENT SEASON moves forward as we prepare to commemorate the birth of Christ. This is not so much a reenactment as a revivification—a remembering that becomes the reality of our lives, the knowledge that God is with us.

Certainly the Communion antiphon points again to the O Antiphon for December 18: "O Mighty Lord… who appeared to Moses in a burning bush." Like that burning bush, God's presence among us, Emmanuel, never burns out. In situations of great joy God is burningly present with us. In situations of difficulty where we have been betrayed or hurt, at the hour of our death, God's presence continues to appear to us and is never extinguished. Emmanuel is a God who desires to be with us in the middle of our chaos so that we are not afraid and never alone, a God who comes to redeem us with an outstretched arm that holds us tightly.

As Christmas draws closer, we are invited to prepare our hearts and know that, even now, God is present with us. In this we find great comfort: No matter what situation we find ourselves in, we need not be afraid because we are in the presence of God. We stand in the middle of the presence of God and are not afraid because Emmanuel is with us. We are set free from fear because we know we are not alone. Recognizing that gift, then, we can become for one another the living Emmanuel. Our love can burn as brightly and consistently as the burning bush in which God appeared to Moses.

PRACTICE

Pray or sing the O Antiphon for today:

O Leader of the House of Israel,
giver of the Law to Moses on Sinai:
come to rescue us with your mighty power!

O Root of Jesse

JUDGES 13:2–7, 24–25; PSALM 71:3–4, 5–6, 16–17; LUKE 1:5–25

The Dawn from on high will visit us,
guiding our feet in the way of peace.

TODAY'S COMMUNION ANTIPHON comes from the Gospel
of Luke and from the words of Zechariah, the father
of John the Baptist. The image of "the Dawn from
on high" is particularly appealing at this time of year
in the northern hemisphere, when the days have been
getting shorter and shorter until the winter solstice on
December 21. As the darkness is coming and deepening
we are preparing for the birth of light at Christmas. We
pray that Christ, the dawn of the light given to us at
baptism, will continue to shine in our footsteps so that
we may always walk in the way of peace.

The antiphon for evening prayer talks about Christ
as the Root of Jesse's tree, which stands as a great signal
to all the nations. When we are rooted in Christ we are
rooted in an ancestry of many who have gone before us.
We stand in the light of the teachings that come to us

from Scripture, and the teachings that come to us from the wisdom of the Catholic community. We stand in the wisdom of Jesus Christ, the One who becomes for us the person and hope in which we are rooted.

This Advent day we might want to ask ourselves the question, "Where can we celebrate the light of Christ given to us in our baptism?" Perhaps we can be rooted again in that light and in the richness of the baptismal tradition by partaking of the sacrament of reconciliation before we celebrate Christmas. In this sacrament we confess our hopes and desires, and are grounded once more in the Root of Jesse, the Christ.

PRACTICE

Pray or sing the O Antiphon for today:

O Root of Jesse's stem,
sign of God's love for all his people:
come to save us without delay!

O Key of David

ISAIAH 7:10–14; PSALM 24:1–2, 3–4, 5–6; LUKE 1:26–38

The Angel said to Mary:
Behold, you will conceive and bear a son,
and you shall name him Jesus.

YEARS AGO WHEN I was studying at the University of Louvain in Belgium, I visited many churches in the area. One was dedicated to Mary, and in it there was an image of her that was quite shocking. Mary sat on a throne with Jesus on her lap, depicted as a one- or two-year-old child. The child was smiling and waving—but Mary clearly was still pregnant! I thought at first that it might be a statue created by someone during the Protestant Reformation, because many of the Reformation Christians believed that Mary had other children.

As I stood there wondering, the curator of the church came by and I asked him what this was all about. He told me this was an image of Mary as the Mother of the Church, always ready to give birth to Christ. In a real sense, as Christmas approaches, isn't that the wonder of this season? Like Mary, we are called to give birth to Christ in our actions and at all times. Like Mary, we are called to respond, "Let it be with me according to your word" (Luke 1:38).

What gets in the way of us completely surrendering to the will of God? How might we learn to become become Christ-bearers in the world? To begin, perhaps we can allow the Key of David to unlock our hearts and our lives so that we will be freed from the chains of the prisons in which we live and walk in the light that is ours given once more in Jesus, Our Lord and Savior.

PRACTICE

Pray or sing the O Antiphon for today:

O Key of David,
opening the gates of God's eternal Kingdom:
come and free the prisoners of darkness!

O Radiant Dawn

Song of Songs 2:8–14 or Zephaniah 3:14–18;
Psalm 33:2–3, 1–12, 20–21; Luke 1:39–35

Blessed are you who have believed,
that what was spoken to you by the Lord would be fulfilled.

HERE WE ARE in the middle of this darkest day of the year, the shortest day in the northern hemisphere. We are invited to believe in the Son, the one who will bring light. In a wonderful liturgical kind of cosmology, the evening antiphon calls out to the Orient, the Radiant Dawn, the sunrise. We believe that the day of the Lord is rising among us, and even if we sit in the darkness and the shadows of death, we believe that light will shine— the Light of Justice, the Light Eternal.

Mary, our dear sister, was able to believe that even in the darkest experiences she would soon face, God would be with her. And God was there when Joseph, "being a righteous man and unwilling to expose her to public disgrace, planned to dismiss her quietly" (Matthew 1:19), sending an angel to tell Joseph in a dream to take

Mary as his wife. God was there when the neighbors found out about her pregnancy, and no doubt gossiped about her. God was there when Mary and Joseph traveled to Bethlehem for the census, while she was close to giving birth.

We rejoice in Mary, and we are invited to yield our hearts as Mary did, to believe that what we have been given in Christ is the daybreak, the sunrise. We believe fully that God's promise is good, that the darkness itself gives way to light. Soon we will celebrate the dawn of Christmas, at the midnight Mass. In the middle of that night, in darkness, we will celebrate with Mary that what has been spoken to her by the angel is now fulfilled.

PRACTICE

Pray or sing the O Antiphon for today:

O Radiant Dawn,
splendor of eternal light, sun of justice:
come and shine on those who dwell in darkness and
in the shadow of death.

O King of the Nations

1 Samuel 1:24–28; 1 Samuel 2:1, 4–5, 6–7, 8abcd; Luke 1:46–56

My soul proclaims the greatness of the Lord,
for the Almighty has done great things for me.

Today's Communion antiphon takes its text from the Magnificat (Luke 1:46–55), where Mary speaks her exquisite prayer, the song sung at Vespers every night. Mary's greatness comes from her lowliness.

The paradox of Christianity is that in order to be great, we must be lowly. In order to be first we are called to be the last; to become strong we are called to become weak; to find ourselves we are called to lose ourselves. A paradox is not something that you understand with your mind, because the mind will see it as a contradiction in terms. But a paradox is best understood by the heart as something that opens up a whole new pathway of thinking, of being alive and being human. It is both/and.

We, like Mary, find in our lowliness the cause of great rejoicing. It is recognizing that by dying we are given the promise of life. By embracing the cross, we are given the wisdom of the Resurrection. We rejoice in our acknowledgment of the God who does great things for us, we who are formed from the clay of the earth. By giving thanks, we allow ourselves to be open to the transformative gifts that God gives us repeatedly, that in these earthen vessels, these containers made of clay, we, like Mary, may find joy.

Slowly now the days begin to get longer, and the light inches back into our world. Yet the darkness still dominates as we look toward the light of Christmas, when our remembrance of the birth of Jesus will once again gloriously illuminate our lives. With Mary, let us rejoice in the brightness of the Almighty who has done great things for her and will do great things for us as well.

PRACTICE

Pray or sing the O Antiphon for today:

O King of all nations and keystone of the Church: come and save man, whom you formed from the dust!

Emmanuel

MALACHI 3:1–4, 23–24; PSALM 25:4–5, 8–9, 10, 14; LUKE 1:57–66

Behold, I stand at the door and knock:
if anyone hears my voice and opens the door to me,
I will enter his house and dine with him, and he with me.

MY MOTHER, WHO at the time of this writing is ninety-three years old, once said to me, "If I had all the riches or money in the world, I would never be able to afford all that God has given me in my life…free of charge." The one who knocks at the door is coming with all kinds of gifts to give us free of charge, and all we have to do to receive these gifts is open the door. And yet, how often do we refuse to receive such a gift-bearer, our Emmanuel?

In Revelation 3:20 we read, "Listen! I am standing at the door, knocking; if you hear my voice and open the door, I will come in to you and eat with you, and you with me." The One whose presence we have been waiting for during Advent is already knocking at our door, inviting us to open up and eat with him.

Religion is often described as a life journey on which its adherents are looking to find God, and that religious traditions are efforts on the part of humanity to construct ways to get to God. Christianity is not so much a journey to find God, but a call to answer the door and let in the God who has been there all the time. It is not we who are looking out for God, but God who is standing at our door knocking, who wants to come and be with us.

As we end the O Antiphons and prepare to celebrate Christmas Eve tomorrow, let us take some time today to unbar the doors of our hearts because Emmanuel knocks, knocks, knocks. Put your hand on your heart today and feel the very beat of the One who is knocking. Then open the door and see what happens.

PRACTICE

Pray or sing the O Antiphon for today:

O Emmanuel, our King and Giver of Law:
come to save us, Lord our God!

Christmas Eve

2 Samuel 7:1–5, 8–12, 14, 16; Psalm 89, 2–3, 4–5, 27, 29;
Romans 16:25–27; Luke 1:26–38

Blessed be the Lord, the God of Israel!
He has visited his people and redeemed them.

On this Christmas Eve, we again hear the words of
Zechariah proclaimed at the birth of his son, John the
Baptist. These same words are said each day during
morning prayer, at the beginning of the Benedictus.

Pope Francis tells us in his apostolic exhortation
Evangelii Gaudium that Christians are people who
remember. As Christmas Eve dawns many memories
may flood our minds of past Christmas Eves. We may
remember all the wonderful experiences of Christmas
Eve as children, memories of sights and smells, of snow-
falls and the joy of Christmas trees. We remember those
who have been with us on Christmases past, those who
have touched our lives and have gone before us.

Yet there may be memories that need healing. Is there
someone who has harmed us, or a memory of pain from

childhood? Do we have a memory of someone who is sick and dying? As we prepare to celebrate the birth of Jesus, we can ask the Lord to visit us and redeem our memories, heal our memories, so that on Christmas we can place them in the manger of the Christ child. In this way we can freely open our hearts on Christmas day to rejoice in the memory of the One who was born in a manger, died on a cross, and continuously feeds us with his Body and Blood.

As the midnight hour approaches and we greet Christmas day, let us be committed to create new memories, memories that sometimes bless and sometimes burn, the memories that we keep and cherish and bless the Lord for. Our memories take us into a future where we will be gathered around an eternal banquet table and celebrate there forever the visitation of God, Emmanuel, the God who calls us into the holiness and the fullness of life.

PRACTICE
What memories come to mind on this Christmas Eve? What new memories can you make this year?

Christmas Day

ISAIAH 9:1–6; PSALM 96:1–2, 2–3, 11–12, 13; TITUS 2:11–14;
LUKE 2:1–14

The Word became flesh, and we have seen his glory.

BLESSINGS FOR THIS holy feast of Christmas! There are
actually four celebrations of the Eucharist for Christmas:
the Christmas Vigil Mass, celebrated on Christmas Eve
during the evening hours; a Mass during the night,
sometimes celebrated at midnight but often a few hours
earlier; a Mass at dawn; and a celebration during the
day. The Communion antiphons for each of these four
celebrations can be summed up in the antiphon that
we use at the midnight Mass on Christmas, a quote
from John 1:14: "And the Word became flesh and lived
among us, and we have seen his glory, the glory as of a
father's only son, full of grace and truth."

Christmas is all about the glory of God made flesh
in our lives. It is something we have seen with our eyes,
we have heard with our ears, we have touched with
our hands, we have tasted with our mouths, we have

smelled with our noses, we have experienced in all of our physical senses. We have experienced the God who has become physically connected with us. We are the people who walked in darkness and we have seen the glory of God.

There is a story about a mother who puts her little daughter to bed and then leaves the room. Suddenly, the little girl yells, "Mother!" The mother rushes into the room and asks, "What do you want, honey?" The daughter says, "A glass of water," so the mother brings her a glass of water. A few minutes later the daughter cries out again, "Mother!" and the mother runs into the room and asks, "What do you want?" The daughter says, "I need to go to the bathroom" and so she does. Finally the daughter cries out again, "Mother!" and the mother says, "What do you really want?" The little girl says, "I am afraid of the dark." The mother says, "Well, honey, don't you know that God is with you? You don't need to be afraid of the dark." The little daughter then looked at her mother and said, "Yes, I know, but when it is dark like this I need something with skin."

The good news of Christmas is that the Word has become flesh and dwells among us. In the middle of darkness we have seen light.

Christmas is a time when all of our senses are touched. We see Christmas trees. We hear Christmas music. We taste Christmas cookies. We smell pine trees. We are able to touch each other in embraces of affection and forgiveness. Through our five senses we celebrate the great Incarnate Word who loved us so much that he fully engaged in our humanity, in all things but sin.

Christmas is an opportunity for us to rejoice in the Word becoming flesh, to savor this wonderful mystery with all our senses, so that in turn we can go out and be seen and heard and touched and scented and tasted as the living Christ this Christmastime and each day of the new year.

PRACTICE
What is your favorite sensory experience of Christmas? Give thanks to God for that gift today.

Feast of St. Stephen

ACTS 6:8–10; 7:54–59; PSALM 31:3–4, 6 AND 8AB, 16BC, 17;
MATTHEW 10:17–22

As they were stoning Stephen, he called out:
Lord Jesus, receive my spirit.

AS WE CELEBRATE the second day of Christmas, we are
greeted by the first martyr of the Church, Stephen,
whom we hear about in the Acts of the Apostles. He
was a young deacon in the early Church, one of the
seven deacons chosen to assist in supplying resources
and monies to the widows and the poor among the
Christian community. With the deacons serving the
needs of the community, the apostles were free to go
out and preach.

The word *martyr* means "witness," and Stephen is a
noble witness to the fact that Christianity was a persecuted religion. In celebrating his feast day on the first
day of Christmas, the Church says to us, "In the midst
of all the joy of Christmas and the glory of the One

who is being proclaimed, the task of evangelizing is risky business."

As he was dying, not only did Stephen cry out, "Lord Jesus, receive my spirit," but like Jesus on the cross he says, "Forgive them." We are called to give witness by our healing mercy and forgiveness to others. We are called to give witness by giving ourselves over to the service of the poor and disenfranchised. We are called to give witness by our works of justice in places that are unjust and do not offer people their human dignity.

Even today, in the twenty-first century, there are Christian witnesses throughout the world who are martyred for the faith. They are killed most often for their commitment to the cause of the poor and disenfranchised, to the ones that are persecuted and marked as alien.

As Christ commended his spirit to the Father and Stephen commended his spirit to Christ, so let us too commend our spirits to Christ and to one another. Let us be committed to give witness to Christ incarnate among us as fearlessly as St. Stephen, the first martyr of the Church.

PRACTICE

Are you willing to completely surrender your life to Christ? Why or why not?

Feast of St. John, Apostle and Evangelist

1 John 1:1–4; Psalm 97:1–2, 5–6, 11–12; John 20:1a, 2–8

The Word became flesh and made his dwelling among us,
and from his fullness we have all received.

John was the only one of the apostles who was not martyred in blood, but he gave witness to the Good News throughout his entire and very long life. He is what is known as a white martyr, one who witnesses to the faith without being killed for it.

This saint whom we honor today was the one who, as traditionally understood, reclined at the Lord's breast at the Last Supper. He was the beloved apostle, and as the liturgy suggests, the one to whom celestial secrets were revealed. He was the disciple whom Jesus addressed from the cross, in John 19:27: "'Here is your mother.' And from that hour the disciple took her into his own home." So at his home in Ephesus, where legend says he lived and died after the Ascension, Mary also lived with him.

In a sense, we are all invited to be beloved disciples of Jesus; the fullness of Christ is something we have all received. It's been given to the entire cosmos, the entire universe. We are all partakers and sharers in this fullness.

There are two ways in which we can turn to John the Evangelist to inspire us in our own witness to the Good News. One is that we have been given celestial secrets as well, and we can only come to know those secrets if we take the quiet time, the contemplative time, the meditative time to savor these mysteries. Second, in the simplicity of our behavior and lifestyle we witness to the fullness of Christ within us, sharing the very joy that comes forward from us as witnesses to the Gospel.

Like St. John, we can be white martyrs, witnesses to Christ without shedding our blood, but nevertheless writing a Gospel by everything we say and do.

PRACTICE

In what ways do you see yourself as a beloved disciple of Christ?

Feast of the Holy Innocents

1 John 1:5–2:2; Psalm 124:2–34–5,7cd–8; Matthew 2:13–18

Behold those redeemed as the first fruits
of the human race for God and the Lamb,
and who follow the Lamb wherever he goes.

THIS FOURTH DAY of Christmas commemorates the Holy Innocents, the children who were killed by Herod's rage when he realized that the Magi had deceived him. Rather than returning to Herod and telling him where the child was in Bethlehem, they went home by a different route as we hear in the Gospel of Matthew (2:12). In the meantime, an angel appears to Joseph telling him to take Mary and the child Jesus to Egypt, where they live until the death of Herod.

This event has grabbed the imagination of many artists over the centuries, such as Poussin and Rubens. A popular Christmas song, the "Coventry Carol," recounts this event as well.

This day is also known as "Childermas," a term for a custom dating back at least to the Middle Ages.

Sometimes children would take on the role of parents, and parents of their children. (This might be interesting to try today, within limits!) Another practice is to bless children on this day; you can do this simply by making the Sign of the Cross on their forehead, perhaps offering a few words of prayer or blessing as well.

There is also a movement suggested by the Desmond Tutu Center to remember all the holy innocents throughout the world by committing ourselves to mark the Feast of the Holy Innocents once a week, all year long. For instance, if this feast falls on a Tuesday, then every Tuesday in that calendar year would be a day to pray for children who are suffering in this world—from AIDS or child abuse, or children who live in hunger and poverty, or those who are sick.

Let us live in solidarity with those who weep and mourn for their children and for the loss of the holy innocents that happens today, even in our midst.

PRACTICE

Pray for a child today, whether one in your family or community or in the world at large.

Tender Mercy

1 JOHN 2:3–11; PSALM 96:1–2A, 2B–3, 5B–6; LUKE 2:22–35

Through the tender mercy of our God,
the Dawn from on high will visit us.

DECEMBER 29, THE fifth day in the Octave of the Nativity of the Lord, is basically just a simple day in the Octave. There is no major saint or other feast to commemorate, although it is the feast of St. Thomas Becket, the great bishop and martyr. Liturgically, however, it's simply December 29.

The antiphon that leads us through today names the tender mercy of our God, the Dawn from on high who will visit us. We have not heard this antiphon before in Advent. However, like other Communion antiphons this season, it too comes from Luke 1:78, from the great prayer called the Benedictus uttered by Zechariah.

God's tender mercy comes from the very depths of God, from the place where life is given and meted out. One can think of a mother giving birth from that very place at the umbilicus. This is what the antiphon is getting at, the very visceral nature of God's mercy toward us.

Have you ever felt insecure, or like the world was falling apart? Have you ever felt there was something empty, a hole in the middle of your stomach where everything seems to have dropped out? This celebration of Christmas says, "Even in those moments of gut-wrenching fear, when it seems like everything and everyone has left and that you have been abandoned completely, from the depths of God's being we are given mercy." And from the depths of God's heart we are given Christ, who feeds us, for the Dawn from on high has visited us.

Even in the most fearful times and darkest moments, we remember the love of our merciful God, who beckons us with the Good News and the promise of Christ.

PRACTICE
What is your deepest fear? Lay it before the infant Jesus today, confident of his mercy and love.

(The Feast of the Holy Family is celebrated on the Sunday between Christmas and January 1. If there is no Sunday between these two feasts, Holy Family is celebrated on December 30.)

The Family of God

SIRACH 3:2–6, 12–14; PSALM 105:1–2, 3–4, 5–6, 8–9;
COLOSSIANS 3:12–21; LUKE 2:22–40

Our God has appeared on earth, and lived among us.

STARTING BACK IN the late twentieth century and continuing on into this twenty-first century, what we know as family is going through a massive shift. The traditional family of a mother, father, and children has not been the norm for some time now, at least here in the United States. Today more than ever we have single-parent families, interreligious families, interracial families, and same-gender families.

As we celebrate this Feast of the Holy Family, it is important to recognize that the family unit, however it is configured, has a clear task: to provide a stable home for children so that they, like the child Jesus, can grow in wisdom and grace (see Luke 2:40). Families are the place where the next generation of humanity is shaped and formed as these children are brought into the world and live among us. They're given a place of security. They're given a place where this experience of humanity can dwell deeply.

For a family to be holy it must ask itself questions. The first is, how are we doing with generosity, with giving of ourselves to each other, parents to parents, parents to children, children to children, and children to parents? Self-centeredness is not an option here. Second, how much do we open ourselves up to the reality of the discipline that it takes to be a family, to take care of ourselves and the other family members? Third, do we make time for prayer?

With generosity and discipline and prayer, we can build the other virtues and values that allow us to be a strong family, no matter how our family is composed. We will offer to the children of the future the grounding they need to continue to grow as a global family, a human family, so that one day we might stand together as a people rejoicing in the goodness of God.

PRACTICE

What does family mean to you? Say the following Family Prayer in thanksgiving for the gift of family.

A FAMILY PRAYER

O God our Father,
in Jesus you call all Christian families and homes
to be signs of living faith.
By the light of the Holy Spirit,
lead us to be thankful for the gift of faith,
and by that gift
may we grow in our relationship with Jesus, your Son,
and be confident witnesses to Christian hope and joy
to all we meet.
In the name of Jesus Christ our Lord.
Amen.

— *United States Conference of Catholic Bishops*

Grace upon Grace upon Grace

1 John 2:12–17; Psalm 96:7–8a, 8b–9, 10; Luke 2:36–40

From his fullness we have all received,
grace upon grace.

THE COMMUNION ANTIPHON brings us again to the heart of that mystery from the prologue of John's Gospel (1:16): "From his fullness we have all received grace upon grace." One could see the hyperbole in all of this. Hyperbole is a form of speech whereby you exaggerate because the experience you're having is so profound, you need a way of stretching language to the extreme to describe it.

So this Communion antiphon uses a bit of hyperbole. You can hear it almost say, "From his fullness we have all received grace upon grace upon grace upon grace upon grace"—ad infinitum. This sense of grace says that, in this present moment, this here and now time that the mystics speak of as the divine moment, the earthly gifts of bread and wine are transformed into a divine presence. As we stand in this divine presence and receive life, as it comes to us seemingly from a future into this present moment and quickly fades into the past, we begin to be overwhelmed by this experience of grace upon grace.

You might wonder, "What happens when life gets difficult and painful? Can even that be grace?" The Christmas response is yes, grace upon grace upon grace, born into the cold of a Bethlehem midnight or fleeing into Egypt to escape the sword. In all of life's situations, when we get really good at experiencing life as a gift, then everything is grace, even the difficult times.

If we look back at the difficult times with Christmas eyes, with the eyes of grace, we might see that those times may actually have been the ones when we have been most transformed, have grown the most, and have come to know the fullness of God.

PRACTICE

Is there a difficult time in your past that, in retrospect, helped you to grow in a positive way?

New Year's Eve

1 John 2:18–21; Psalm 96:1–2, 11–12, 13; John 1:1–18

*God sent his Only Begotten Son into the world,
so that we might have life through him.*

New Year's Eve, the seventh day in the Octave of Christmas, is also known as St. Sylvester Day. Pope Sylvester I, who died in the year 335 on this day, was the pope during the Council of Nicaea. He was a friend of the Emperor Constantine, and very much involved in the transition from the old Roman Empire, where Christians were terrorized and dominated, into a new empire where Christianity was relished and cared for.

The Communion antiphon today can be seen as kind of a summary of the whole year, as we again read 1 John 4:9, "God sent his only Son into the world so that we might live through him." The Gospel of John continues the teaching of this verse, by telling us that we have not only life, but life in abundance, a new life, a fullness of life and a completeness of life. Today, at the close of the year, we look forward to another year of life, a new year of grace, that we might have life in Christ, through Christ, and with Christ.

What might we do to celebrate new life today? Perhaps this is a good day to clean out the clutter—clutter of thoughts and clutter of possessions and clutter of e-mails and clutter of text messages that we don't need—and get rid of all of that clutter to make way for new life.

I recall visiting my mother's hometown outside of Naples, Italy, one New Year's Eve. At 11:50 P.M., ten minutes before the midnight, people began throwing out pots, pans, plates, clothes, all kinds of household goods and clutter that were no longer needed. They were actually throwing these things out the window and celebrating with the noise and the clatter of getting rid of old stuff. Miraculously, by morning, all the streets were cleared, meticulously clean. The New Year had begun.

Practice

What do we need to get rid of so that we might have new life in Christ?

JANUARY 1

Solemnity of Mary, the Holy Mother of God

NUMBERS 6:22–27; PSALM 67:2–3, 5, 6, 8; GALATIANS 4:4–7;
LUKE 2:16–21

Jesus Christ is the same yesterday, today, and for ever.

IN HIS ENCYCLICAL *Evangelii Gaudium*, Pope Francis calls Mary "the star of the new evangelization." She is indeed the one who proclaims Jesus Christ the same yesterday, today, and forever. Mary's very presence among us is an encouragement for the whole Church, as we begin a new year, to proclaim the Incarnate One in our words and in our actions.

The New Evangelization being taught by the Church over the past few years is different from the "old" evangelization, which was focused more on work done by priests and sisters, by missionary religious throughout the world. But as we read so clearly in this particular apostolic exhortation and in the writings of the previous popes—John Paul II and Benedict XVI—the New Evangelization is something that we all do together, the whole Church. All the baptized are being called to evangelize as they continue the journey of faith.

As we begin the new year, we are invited to commit ourselves anew to proclaiming, with Mary, the joy of the gospel of Jesus Christ. Mary is the inspiration for the whole Church to lead us into proclaiming Christ. She leads the way and helps us proclaim the message of salvation, and enables us to become evangelizers in the new year. Her example shows that we proclaim the gospel in our actions through love and tenderness. It is the way of mercy, the way of humility, a way that recognizes that in all our efforts, God is working through us. It is the recognition of an unspeakable hope that God will work within us a new creation, as he did through Mary.

As we start this new year, let us look for ways in which our hearts are still proud, or areas where we are called to be merciful or forgive others. Because January 1 is also a day of prayer for peace in the world, perhaps there is an opportunity to evangelize by reaching out, forgiving, and reconciling with members of our family or our friends.

PRACTICE

May our actions today give life to the words of a popular hymn: "Let there be peace on earth, and let it begin with me."

(As a special blessing for the New Year, say the Prayer to Mary written for the Year of Faith [October 2012—November 2013] and found on page 96 of this book.)

We Are the Star

1 JOHN 2:22–28; PSALM 98: 1, 2–3AB, 3CD–4; JOHN 1:19–28

We have seen his glory, the glory of an only Son
coming from the Father,
filled with grace and truth.

EVEN THOUGH THERE are still almost two weeks left in the Christmas season, for all practical purposes most of us have left the holidays behind and have gone back to Ordinary Time. Yet as the antiphon reads today, "We have seen his glory"; over the course of Christmas and the Advent season, we have become a people transformed by the presence of God-with-us, Emmanuel. We have been filled with the grace of incarnation, and made whole by the truth of the living Word who dwells among us.

And so we go out into the world to share this Good News, with the memory of Christmas stamped on our souls. We are now the angels that the shepherds heard at Jesus's birth, the star the wise men followed to Bethlehem.

PRACTICE

How will your light shine in the world today?

Sinners, but Saved

1 John 2:29—3:6; Psalm 98 1, 3cd–4, 5–6; John 1:29–34

Because of that great love of his with which God loved us,
he sent his Son in the likeness of sinful flesh.

Most of us don't think of our bodies as "sinful flesh," especially since in 1 Corinthians 6:19 we are told, "your body is a temple of the Holy Spirit within you…." And yet we are indeed sinners, with the exception of Jesus. It's part of what it means to be human.

Why would Jesus become human like us? Certainly to redeem us from sin, but also to show us the way to live in a world filled with conflict and chaos. God sent us his Son who guides us in the way of peace, living righteously and with a blameless heart. Indeed, Jesus showed us how to live as human beings with the presence of God within us. That is the ultimate love.

Practice
Take some time today to thank God for the gift of being human.

Come and See

1 John 3:7–10; Psalm 98:1, 7–8, 9; John 1:35–42

*That life which was with the Father became visible,
and has appeared to us.*

Today's Gospel echoes the wonderful theme of the antiphon, the Incarnation that became visible and appeared to us: "[The two disciples] said to him, 'Rabbi' (which translated means Teacher), 'where are you staying?' He said to them, 'Come and see'" (1:38). This is more than an invitation to take a look at the house Jesus is in; it is a call to follow Jesus and learn from him.

We have seen the glory of God revealed in the birth of Jesus. We have heard the angels rejoicing and the shepherds running to see what has occurred in the manger. We have been drawn into the life that was with the Father, and appeared to us here, in our world. In the real presence of Jesus's Body and Blood, we see Christ revealed each time we receive Holy Communion.

Practice

What do you "see" when you receive Holy Communion?

Hope Lives

1 JOHN 3:11–21; PSALM 100:1B–2, 3, 4, 5; JOHN 1:43–51

God so loved the world that he gave his Only Begotten Son,
so that all who believe in him may not perish, but may
have eternal life.

TODAY'S ANTIPHON IS a verse that has reached a place in the public consciousness. We see fans at football games holding up signs that read "John 3:16," and find this verse on billboards along the highways of this country. It's a message that speaks of hope, the hope of Jesus and of the eternal life he brings.

Most of us are winding down from the celebration of Christmas. Our decorations may be put away; the presents we received have become part of our daily lives. But the glow from the event we remember at Christmas, the birth of Jesus in our world, stays imprinted on our hearts, feeding the hope that he brought into this world with his life, death, and Resurrection.

PRACTICE

What can you do to keep Christmas hope alive in your heart?

The "Aha!" Moment

Isaiah 60:1–6; Psalm 72:1–2, 7–8, 10–11, 12–13;
Ephesians 3:2–3a, 5–6; Matthew 2:1–12

*We have seen his star in the East,
and have come with gifts to adore the Lord.*

THE TWELFTH DAY of Christmas is known as Feast of the Epiphany of the Lord. The music of the angelic choir that guided the shepherds to the infant Jesus as he lay in a manger has now become the star leading the Magi to that same child.

Epiphany means a manifestation of God, a *theophany*. We might say it's our "Aha!" moment about God. Traditionally, this day actually celebrated three moments of epiphany, when God becomes present to us. First, it celebrated the Magi who read the stars and knew that something magnificent had happened in the cosmos. The second moment is at Jesus's Baptism by John, when God the Father says, "This is my beloved Son."

The third moment is when Jesus changed water into wine at the wedding feast in Cana. The husband and wife would have been deeply embarrassed by running out of wine, but Jesus helped them, and thus this event became his first miracle, or epiphany. (When I asked a student in my class once what the moral of this story was, he said, "When you're having a wedding make sure you invite Jesus.")

The Epiphany, with its threefold mystery, celebrates the manifestation of God to the nations, so all the nations will walk in the light, as we hear in the Communion antiphon for the Vigil Mass of the Epiphany: "The brightness of God illumined the holy city Jerusalem, and the nations will walk by its light." We come to the altar, and like the Magi and John the Baptist and the bride and groom in Cana, we are dazzled by the epiphany of God. On this twelfth day of Christmas may we consider this an opportunity to allow the spirit of Christmas to become incarnated in us so that we become the living star, the living epiphany.

PRACTICE
How can our lives be a revelation of God to others?

Called by Christ

ISAIAH 42:1–4, 6–7; PSALM 29:1–2, 3–4, 9–10; ACTS 10:34–38;
MATTHEW 3:13–17

Behold the One of whom John said:
I have seen and testified that this is the Son of God.

SO WE COME to the liturgical end of the Christmas season, the Feast of the Baptism of the Lord. Before we consider this feast, though, let's take a look again at the meditation for the First Sunday of Advent. There, the Gospel of Luke for Year C speaks of the destruction of the whole world; the planets will come down and the great cataclysmic *eschaton* will arrive. Then, as the Communion antiphon reads that day, "The Lord will bestow his bounty and our earth shall yield its increase."

Here at the end of the Christmas season the skies do open and a voice does speak from the clouds, and the Spirit descends on Jesus. It is a great manifestation of the Trinity as the cosmic forces are joined with Jesus, who enters into the waters of death and emerges from the waters of life. There, in the midst of it all, the earth yields its fruits. The bounty that we proclaim at the beginning of Advent now comes to its great fruition not in a baby but in a beloved Son. As the glory of the Lord is made manifest in the River Jordan, a new creation comes forth; the earth has brought forth its bounty in Jesus Christ.

The Greek word used in the Gospel when God refers to the Son is *paidiske*, which means not only a child but a servant. In his baptism, Jesus is shown to be both the Son of God and the servant of God. By our own baptism, we are acknowledged as children of God and, like Jesus, called to be servants and go out to the ends of the earth, proclaiming the manifestation of God— Jesus, incarnate in us and in the world.

In the early days of both the Eastern and the Western churches, the end of the Christmas season was a time to baptize neophytes, as is done now at the Easter Vigil. This feast was considered Easter in the wintertime. Even today, in many of the Orthodox churches people go out to the lakes and the oceans and bless the water, then sprinkle this water over one another to bring an end to the Christmas season.

We have come to the end of yet another Advent and Christmas season. The richness of the Communion antiphons has given us a different perspective on this season, one that I pray has helped you grow in faith, hope, and the love of our merciful and generous God. May you be led more richly and more fully each week to the Eucharistic Table of the Lord, inspired by the meditations in this little book. God bless!

PRACTICE

Do you know the date of your baptism? If not, find out and celebrate that day each year.

Prayer to Mary

Mary, Virgin and Mother,
you who, moved by the Holy Spirit,
welcomed the word of life
in the depths of your humble faith:
as you gave yourself completely to the Eternal One,
help us to say our own "yes"
to the urgent call, as pressing as ever,
to proclaim the good news of Jesus.
Filled with Christ's presence,
you brought joy to John the Baptist,
making him exult in the womb of his mother.
Brimming over with joy,
you sang of the great things done by God.
Standing at the foot of the cross
with unyielding faith,
you received the joyful comfort of the resurrection,
and joined the disciples in awaiting the Spirit
so that the evangelizing Church might be born.
Obtain for us now a new ardour born of the resurrection,
that we may bring to all the Gospel of life

which triumphs over death.
Give us a holy courage to seek new paths,
that the gift of unfading beauty
may reach every man and woman.
Virgin of listening and contemplation,
Mother of love, Bride of the eternal wedding feast,
pray for the Church, whose pure icon you are,
that she may never be closed in on herself
or lose her passion for establishing God's kingdom.
Star of the new evangelization,
help us to bear radiant witness to communion,
service, ardent and generous faith,
justice and love of the poor,
that the joy of the Gospel
may reach to the ends of the earth,
illuminating even the fringes of our world.
Mother of the living Gospel,
wellspring of happiness for God's little ones,
pray for us.
Amen. Alleluia!

—*Evangelii Gaudium*, 288

ABOUT THE AUTHOR

Richard N. Fragomeni, a priest of the Diocese of Albany, New York, is an associate professor of liturgy and preaching at the Catholic Theological Union in Chicago. He is a popular speaker at major Catholic conferences, parish retreats, and missions, and is the author of *Come to the Feast*.